ALSO BY FR. MARK GORING, CC

- Treasure in Heaven
A 40-Day; ten minutes a day prayer guide

- In His Zone
7 Principles for Thriving in Solitude

St. Joseph the Protector

A Nine-day Preparation for Entrustment to St. Joseph

FR. MARK GORING, CC

Companions of the Cross

Companions of the Cross
199 Bayswater Avenue
Ottawa, Ontario K1Y 2G5
****

1949 Cullen Boulevard
Houston, TX 77023

www.companionscross.org

St. Joseph the Protector
by Fr. Mark Goring, CC

Designed by Jaroz.

cover photo: stained glass window in St. Columbkille
Cathedral, Pembroke, ON
artist: Guido Nincheri, windows installed in 1954
used with permission.

In Memory of Fr. Bob Bedard, CC
July 17, 1929 – October 6, 2011

This booklet is a nine-day preparation for entrustment to St. Joseph.
Each day read one chapter and then pray the Memorare to St. Joseph
followed by an Our Father, Hail Mary and a Glory be.
On the last day entrust yourself to St. Joseph by praying the prayer of
entrustment on p. 55

Nihil obstat: Rev. Richard Jaworski, CC

                              Censor deputatus

Imprimatur: Most Rev. Terrence Prendergast, S.J.

                              Archbishop of Ottawa

                              September 8, 2014

Contents

Introduction

*Saint Joseph urged me to have a constant devotion to him.
He himself told me to recite three prayers [the Our Father,
Hail Mary and Glory be] and the Memorare once every day.
He looked at me with great kindness and gave me to know
how much he is supporting this work [of mercy]. He has
promised me this special help and protection. I recite the
requested prayers every day and feel his special protection.*[1]-
St. Faustina

*I prayed to St. Joseph to watch over me. From my childhood,
my devotion to him was mingled with my love for the Blessed
Virgin. Each day I recited the prayer, "O Saint Joseph, father
and protector of virgins." It seemed to me that I was well
protected and completely sheltered from every danger.* [2]- St.
Therese of Lisieux

After the Blessed Virgin Mary, there is no saint in the Catholic Church
who is more highly honored than St. Joseph. As Catholics, we love St.
Joseph. We have a great devotion to him. The Church celebrates a number
of feasts in his honor. We invoke St. Joseph in the Eucharistic Prayer and
the Divine Praises. St. Joseph has many beautiful titles. He is called the

1   *Sister Maria Faustina Kowalkska, Diary of St. Faustina Maria
     Kowalkska: Divine Mercy in my Soul (2003), para. 1203*
2   *St. Therese of Lisieux, Autography: Story of a Soul, Chapter VI*

Protector of Holy Church, Terror of Demons, Patron of the Dying, Pillar of Families, Foster Father of the Son of God, and Spouse of the Mother of God, to name a few.

Devotion to St. Joseph is meant to complement devotion to Our Lady. This little book will help readers learn more about the foster father of Jesus. It is also a guide for preparing readers to entrust themselves to St. Joseph. When we entrust ourselves to St. Joseph, we are imitating Jesus and Mary who entrusted themselves to this just man. Those who have a devotion to St. Joseph, like St. Faustina, "feel his special protection." St. Joseph was the protector and guardian of Our Lord and Our Blessed Mother. He is Protector of the Holy Church. He can also be our protector.

DAY 1
Man of Silence

───────────── ⚜ ─────────────

...be as one who knows and yet holds his tongue.[3]

In the Bible, not one of Joseph's words is recorded. He is completely silent. He is the Silent Man, and this silence should catch our attention. It is easy to look at Joseph's silence and dismiss him, to think that the foster father of Jesus is nothing but a minor character in the story of salvation. We could think that because Joseph is silent, he didn't know what was going on, that he wasn't aware of the mysteries surrounding him. But I invite you to not be fooled by his silence. The silence of St. Joseph should speak loudly to us.

Ten things Joseph knew

What did St. Joseph know about the mysteries that surrounded him? If we look at Sacred Scripture, it should be obvious to us that he knew a lot. Here are ten things that Joseph knew:

1. *Joseph knew how to be led by God.* More than once, an angel visited this humble carpenter in a dream. Joseph did not respond to these dreams by being disturbed, confused, or overwhelmed. He simply did what he was told to do.

2. *Joseph knew a heavenly plan was being carried out.* God was

....

3   *Sirach 32:8*

13

not only directing Joseph's life, but also fulfilling His promise of salvation for all people. Through the guidance of angels, Joseph could see that a great work of God was beginning.

3. *Joseph knew that Jesus was conceived by the Holy Spirit.* He was told in a dream by an angel, "that which *is conceived in her is of the Holy Spirit.*"[4] This mystery was only revealed to a few people. Throughout Jesus' life, everyone assumed that he was the natural son of Mary and Joseph. The awesome reality that Jesus was conceived by the Holy Spirit was hidden from almost everyone, but not from Joseph.

4. *Joseph knew that the child would save God's people.* This too was revealed to the foster father of Jesus in a dream. *"She will bear a son and you are to name him Jesus, because he will save his people from their sins."*[5]

5. *Joseph knew that the child had a great mission.* Jesus' mission was made obvious at the time of His conception and after birth; it was confirmed when He was presented in the Temple. Simeon and Anna proclaimed both the identity and the mission of the newborn Savior.[6] Luke tells us that *"his father and his mother marveled at what was said about him."*[7]

6. *Joseph knew that the child had come for all people.* He had come not just as the Savior of the Chosen People, but as Simeon said, *"a light of revelation to the Gentiles."*[8] "Gentiles" implies all people. Joseph knew that the person working next to him in his carpentry shop was no ordinary man.

7. *Joseph knew that many were expecting the coming of the Messiah, including Herod.* When the Magi came to Herod looking for the

. . . .

4   *Matthew 1:20*
5   *Matthew 1:21 (NAB)*
6   *Luke 2:25-38*
7   *Luke 2:33*
8   *Luke 2:32*

King of the Jews, *"assembling all the chief priests and the scribes of the people, he inquired of them where the Messiah was to be born."*[9] All of Jerusalem was anticipating the coming of the Messiah.[10] An angel appeared to Joseph in a dream and told him to flee to Egypt because Herod was trying to kill the child.[11] Did the husband of Mary know that the child entrusted to him was indeed the Messiah? It is very likely that he did.

8. *Joseph knew Our Lady well.* He was her husband. They not only shared daily life, but they also walked together in faith. Our Lady is the Immaculate Conception, the most grace filled human being ever created. As her husband, Joseph would have been the one with whom our Blessed Mother would have shared her joys and sorrows and the thoughts of her heart. Imagine the privilege of sharing life with Mary!

9. *Joseph knew Jesus well.*   He was the man closest to Jesus. As his earthly father, he was present when our Savior was born. So often he held the Divine Child in his arms, next to his heart. He provided food for the One who would feed the hungry crowds. He helped Him to learn to walk and taught Him the carpentry trade. Joseph had the privilege of living and working with the Savior!

10. *Joseph knew the teachings of Our Lord.* The humble carpenter was taught by the Master Himself. When Jesus was found in the Temple at the age of twelve, he was asking questions, which is a very Jewish way of teaching. Rather than simply telling things to one's students, the teacher asks questions to open the student's mind to the truths he wishes to impart. Jesus is the Divine Teacher. The finding of Our Lord in the temple indicates the beginning of Jesus' teaching ministry. From the age of twelve until Jesus began His public ministry, Joseph and Mary sat at the

. . . .

9   *Matthew 2:4*
10   *Matthew 2:3*
11   *Matthew 2:13*

15

feet of the Master and received His Divine teaching. Joseph was filled with Our Lord's Heavenly wisdom.

So what did this Silent Man know? Along with the Blessed Virgin Mary, Joseph may have known more about God's plan of salvation than anyone else. There is such a contrast between what Joseph knew and his silence. It was this very silence that was the essence of his mission.

Silence was part of the humble carpenter's unique mission. Unlike the disciples, who were called to make Christ known to the world, Joseph's mission was to hide the child, to veil and protect Jesus until his hour had come. Joseph had to hide Jesus from Herod who sought to kill him. Throughout his childhood, Joseph continued to keep Jesus' identity secret until the day of his manifestation. He fulfilled his mission well because as Jesus began his public ministry, people asked, *"Isn't this the carpenter's son?"*[12] For this mission, God chose and prepared someone who was able to keep silence. Being silent and drawing attention away from himself was Joseph's primary charism. St. Joseph is the man of silence.

St. Joseph and his mission are prefigured in the Old Testament. The Ark of the Covenant gives us a foreshadowing of this great patriarch. As the Chosen People were journeying out of Egypt to the Promised Land, Moses was commanded by the Lord to build the Ark of the Covenant. The Ark of the Covenant was a golden vessel that held Aaron's staff, the stone tablets on which the Ten Commandments were written, and a jar containing manna.[13] In a mysterious way, it was also the place of God's presence among His People. The presence of God in the Ark of the Covenant prefigured Jesus, who is Emmanuel, *"God with us."*[14] The golden vessel foreshadowed Mary, God's chosen vessel who would carry Jesus in her womb. She is the Ark of the New Covenant. The Ark of the Covenant was veiled, hidden from the sight of men by a tent. Who is the tent? St. Joseph. He was the one who veiled, who hid the Messiah until his hour had come.

....

12   *Matthew 13:55*
13   *Hebrews 9:4*
14   *Matthew 1:23*

16

St. Joseph, Man of Silence, pray for us!

Memorare to St. Joseph

Remember, O most chaste spouse of the Virgin Mary, that never was it known that anyone who implored your help and sought your intercession were left unassisted.
Full of confidence in your power I fly unto you and beg your protection. Despise not O Guardian of the Redeemer my humble supplication, but in your bounty, hear and answer me. Amen.

Our Father, Hail Mary, Glory be...

DAY 2
Foster Father of Jesus

⸺⸺⸺⸺⸺ ✎ ⸺⸺⸺⸺⸺

In the course of his hidden life in Nazareth Jesus stayed in the silence of an ordinary existence. This allows us to enter into fellowship with him in the holiness to be found in a daily life marked by prayer, simplicity, work and family love. His obedience to Mary and to Joseph, his foster father, is an image of his filial obedience to the Father. Mary and Joseph accepted with faith the mystery of Jesus even though they did not always understand it.[15]
- Compendium of the Catechism of the Catholic Church

Let us now look at the fatherhood of St. Joseph. Is it proper to refer to Joseph as Jesus' father? There are a few things we need to consider. Firstly, Our Lord's genealogy is traced through St. Joseph.[16] Secondly, St. Luke does refer to Joseph as Jesus' father: *"The child's father and mother were amazed at what was said about him."*[17] When Jesus was found in the Temple, Mary refers to Joseph as Jesus' father: *"Son, why have you done this to us? Your father and I have been looking for you with great anxiety."*[18] At the same time, it must be highlighted that Jesus is ultimately the Son of God the Father, which Jesus makes clear at the age of 12 in the Temple. So yes, Joseph is father to Jesus, but only a temporal father with

· ·

15   *Compendium of the Catechism of the Catholic Church, No. 104*
16   *Matthew 1:17, Luke 3:23-38*
17   *Luke 2:33*
18   *Luke 2:48*

temporal authority. Thus, it is a common tradition in the Church to refer to Joseph as the foster father of Jesus.

It is important to recognize that Joseph was very much a present father. He was present at Our Lord's birth. With Our Lady, he presented the infant Jesus in the Temple. He searched for Jesus when He was missing in Jerusalem at the age of 12. As the guardian of Mary and Jesus, Joseph diligently watched over his family.

Not only was he present in those formative years, but he also had the privilege of sharing life with Jesus into His adulthood. Scripture indicates that Jesus and Joseph worked together as carpenters. When Jesus began his public ministry, people's first reaction to him was, "*Is this not the carpenter?*"[19], and "*Is this not the carpenter's son?*"[20] We know that Jesus was a carpenter, and it seems pretty evident that He learned His carpentry trade from His dad, Joseph.

Joseph was the one chosen by God to be the recipient of Jesus' honor. The fourth commandment says, "*You shall honor your father and mother.*[21]" Certainly Jesus, a faithful Jew and the Son of God, fulfilled this commandment perfectly. Jesus honored his parents. Our Lord gave Joseph more than a legal observance of the law; He honored Joseph wholeheartedly. Jesus is the one who wants to give of Himself in love. We see this in the Eucharist; He gives us His very Heart, His whole being, His whole self. So just imagine Jesus, God the Son, the Second Person of the Trinity, giving of Himself to Joseph and Mary. Never were a father and mother so lovingly and perfectly honored as Mary and Joseph were.

As we reflect on the fatherhood of St. Joseph, we must remember that any call from God is first and foremost a call to be close to God. For example, when God calls a man to the priesthood, the call is first a call to union with Christ and secondly to fulfill his priestly roles. When a person is called to the married life, the call is again first a call to be close to God and secondly

....

19   Mark 6:3
20   Matthew 13:55
21   Exodus 20:12

to one's spouse. Joseph's calling was not just a duty or a function; it was a relationship. The humble carpenter was called to be a good father to Jesus, which required him to have a loving relationship with Our Lord. Joseph was not just a provider; he was truly a father. Joseph was given a mission but more importantly he was given a relationship.

As father, St. Joseph played a primary role in forming Jesus' humanity. Jesus, a divine person with a divine nature, assumed a human nature and therefore needed to be formed in His humanity. He needed to learn how to walk, to speak, to read, and eventually how to be a man. As Scripture says, "*Jesus increased in wisdom and in stature and in favor with God and man.*"[22] We know that the man who was chosen for the lofty task of forming Jesus was St. Joseph. Not only was he chosen, but he was also prepared for this task. As God chose and prepared the Blessed Virgin Mary to be the mother of the Lord Jesus, so too, God chose and prepared Joseph. In Jeremiah we hear, "*Before I formed you in the womb I knew you and before you were born I consecrated you. I appointed you a prophet to the nations.*"[23] So too, Joseph was consecrated and appointed from the womb. Jesus would have spoken with the same dialect as Joseph and would have practiced carpentry as Joseph did. Jesus would have had some of Joseph's mannerisms and personality traits. Joseph modeled manhood for Jesus. Our Lord loved his earthly father and learned from him.

Jesus in His humanity became like Joseph. Jesus in His divinity is one with the Father. Jesus' mission was to reveal the Father and to make Him known. He says, "*Whoever has seen me has seen the Father.*"[24] Jesus Himself draws the analogy of a son learning from and practicing a trade like his father. "*My Father is at work until now, so I am at work.... A son cannot do anything on his own, but only what he sees his father doing; for what he does, his son will do also. For the Father loves his Son and shows him everything that he himself does.*"[25] Jesus, who was a carpenter, was familiar with how a trade was passed on. I am sure He was thinking of

. . . .

22   Luke 2:52
23   Jeremiah 1:5
24   John 14:9
25   John 5:17,19-20

His foster father as He used this image to describe His relationship with His Heavenly Father. Joseph reflected the Fatherhood of God as he loved Jesus and showed him everything he knew.

Like Our Lady, Joseph was docile to the will of God. The foundation of his fatherhood was a profound poverty of spirit and a radical surrender. Joseph's greatness was in emptying himself so God could work through him. Joseph understood the ultimate fatherhood of God the Father. In this way, the humble carpenter became a worthy model of manhood to the Savior of the world.

St. Joseph, Foster Father of the Son of God, pray for us!

Memorare to St. Joseph

Remember, O most chaste spouse of the Virgin Mary, that never was it known that anyone who implored your help and sought your intercession were left unassisted.
Full of confidence in your power I fly unto you and beg your protection. Despise not O Guardian of the Redeemer my humble supplication, but in your bounty, hear and answer me. Amen.

Our Father, Hail Mary, Glory be...

DAY 3
Joseph's Trial and Annunciation

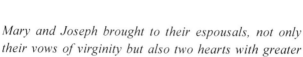

Mary and Joseph brought to their espousals, not only their vows of virginity but also two hearts with greater torrents of love than had ever before coursed through human breasts. No husband and wife ever loved one another so much as Joseph and Mary [26] - Bishop Fulton J. Sheen

The Blessed Virgin Mary was visited by an angel and invited to say "yes" to God's plan. This was Our Lady's Annunciation. Likewise, St. Joseph was visited by an angel and asked for his assent to be the foster father of Jesus and the husband of Mary. This can be referred to as Joseph's annunciation. In the Gospel of Matthew we hear:

"Now the birth of Jesus Christ took place in this way. When his mother Mary had been betrothed to Joseph, before they came together she was found to be with child of the Holy Spirit; and her husband Joseph, being a just man and unwilling to put her to shame, resolved to divorce her quietly. But as he considered this, behold, an angel of the Lord appeared to him in a dream, saying, 'Joseph, son of David, do not fear to take Mary your wife, for that which is conceived in her is of the Holy Spirit; she will bear a son, and you shall call his name Jesus, for he will save his people from their sins.' [...] When Joseph woke from sleep, he did as the angel of

. . . .
26   *Archbishop Fulton Sheen, The World's First Love, Chapter 7*

the Lord commanded him; he took his wife. "[27]

In the litany of St. Joseph, one of the invocations is "Joseph Most Obedient." One of the scriptures that points to Joseph's immediate and unquestioning obedience is his response to his annunciation. *"When Joseph woke from sleep, he did as the angel of the Lord commanded him. "*[28] Joseph always responded to God's commands with perfect obedience. He simply did what the Lord commanded.

Some might question Joseph's obedience by pointing to his resolution to divorce Mary when he finds her to be with child. This difficult situation for Joseph is referred to as St. Joseph's trial. During his trial, Joseph went through the trying experience of not understanding what God was doing. Until his annunciation, Joseph was left in the dark and had to wait for the Lord to reveal to him the mystery being carried out through Mary. This trial was necessary in God's plan, and Joseph did not falter in his obedience throughout the trial.

One aspect of Joseph's trial would have been his inability to comprehend the pregnancy of a woman whose integrity he could not question. Joseph, perhaps more than anyone else, knew Our Lady's unparalleled holiness. As Catholics, we understand that Our Lady is the Immaculate Conception, conceived without original sin. Joseph's annunciation clarified for him the profound mystery of the Blessed Virgin Mary.

Joseph's trial is an example of how difficult it can be to wait on the Lord's timing. Sometimes the Lord does not reveal to us immediately the path that we must take; the Lord simply asks us to wait and trust. Joseph would not have taken Mary to be his wife and assumed care of the child without being sure that this was God's will. After Joseph had made the decision to divorce Mary, but before he had acted on that decision, the Gospel tells us that he spent time "considering" it. We can be sure that the "considering" by this just man would have taken place while immersed in deep prayer. It is during this consideration that the angel of the Lord comes to Joseph

. . . .

27   *Matthew 1:18-21, 24*
28   *Matthew 1:24*

in a dream. With his annunciation, Joseph was given peace and clarity, which allowed him to proceed. He immediately acted by taking Mary into his home.

Another aspect of Joseph's trial is his fear to take Mary as his wife. The angel that appears to him specifically tells him, *"Do not fear to take Mary your wife."* [29] The fear that Joseph is struggling with is a holy fear which is different from being scared or lacking faith. Joseph was a man of courage. He was afraid because he understood that he could not make any decisions without the assurance of knowing he was doing God's will. Like the Hebrew people, who were led through the desert by the pillar of cloud and fire, Joseph did not proceed unless he knew the Lord was leading him. Years later, this holy fear would guide Joseph to move to Nazareth, and by so doing fulfill the Scriptures. [30]

Some of the early church fathers have suggested that the reason Joseph hesitated to take Mary as his wife was that he did not want to be presumptuous. Joseph, the model of humility, would not have presumed to be the foster father of this holy child unless heaven invited him to be. Perhaps Joseph perceived the Lord's presence within Mary, as did Elizabeth. When Mary visited her cousin, Elizabeth, upon hearing Mary's voice, Elizabeth proclaimed, *"How does this happen to me, that the mother of my Lord should come to me?"* [31] Peter, too, felt unworthy to be in the presence of his Lord. When he first met Jesus he said, *"Depart from me, Lord, for I am a sinful man."* [32] Many saints and mystics believed that Joseph, in his humility, would not presume to be the foster father of the Son of God unless God specifically told him to. And God of course did tell him.

In Joseph's trial, we also see God's perfect timing. Jesus was conceived during the time of betrothal. In Jesus' time, marriage took place in three stages according to the Jewish custom. The first stage was what we would

· ·

29   *Matthew 1:20*
30   *Matthew 2:22-23*
31   *Luke 1:43*
32   *Luke 5:8*

call the time of engagement. The second stage was the betrothal in which the couple was legally married but not yet living together. During this time the husband would prepare a home for he and his wife to live in. We know that Mary was legally married to Joseph because the angel refers to Mary as Joseph's wife.[33] Finally, in the third stage of marriage, the husband takes his wife into his home. It was in the "in between" stage of betrothal that Jesus was conceived in the womb of Mary by the Holy Spirit. *"When his mother Mary had been betrothed to Joseph, before they came together, she was found to be with child of the Holy Spirit."*[34]

Conception during the time of betrothal was perfect timing and so too was Joseph's annunciation. The fact that Joseph resolved to divorce Mary quietly has made it obvious to all that Joseph was not the natural father of Jesus. There could hardly be more convincing evidence that Joseph was not a part of Jesus' conception, than the fact that he resolved to divorce her. It could be that Joseph's resolve to divorce Mary was necessary, and that God waited for Joseph to make this decision before inviting him into the mystery of the Incarnation. Had Jesus been conceived after they had come together, skeptics would have easily dismissed the truth of Jesus' incarnation. Had Jesus been conceived before the betrothal, Jesus would have been conceived out of wedlock. God wanted His Son to be conceived within the context of marriage, to a couple that were married according to God's Law. When Jesus was conceived, Mary and Joseph were legally married. The timing could not have been better. God saw to it when Jesus grew up, he would be considered the son of Mary and Joseph. Scripture tells us that when a couple is married, they are one. We could then say that when Jesus was conceived in the womb of the Blessed Mother, he was given not only to one person but to a couple; to Mary and Joseph.

Joseph was indeed called by God to be the husband of Mary and foster father of Jesus. Theirs was truly a marriage made in heaven, confirmed by God's own angels. Even the most perfect marriage has to go through its times of trial and uncertainty, giving us all confidence that God is always with us, mysteriously fulfilling His purposes.

. . . .

33   *Matthew 1:20*
34   *Matthew 1:18*

St. Joseph, Spouse of the Mother of God, pray for us!

Memorare to St. Joseph

Remember, O most chaste spouse of the Virgin Mary, that never was it known that anyone who implored your help and sought your intercession were left unassisted.
Full of confidence in your power I fly unto you and beg your protection. Despise not O Guardian of the Redeemer my humble supplication, but in your bounty, hear and answer me. Amen.

Our Father, Hail Mary, Glory be...

Day 4
Patron of Contemplatives

————————⌘————————

The silence of St. Joseph is given a special emphasis. His silence is steeped in contemplation of the mystery of God in an attitude of total availability to the divine desires. It is a silence thanks to which Joseph, in unison with Mary, watches over the Word of God, known through the Sacred Scriptures, continuously comparing it with the events of the life of Jesus; a silence woven of constant prayer, a prayer of blessing of the Lord, of the adoration of his holy will and of unreserved entrustment to his providence. It is no exaggeration to think that it was precisely from his "father" Joseph that Jesus learned – at the human level – that steadfast interiority which is a presupposition of authentic justice…. Let us allow ourselves to be "filled" with St. Joseph's silence! In a world that is often too noisy, that encourages neither recollection nor listening to God's voice[35]. - Pope Benedict XVI, Angelus

As a man of silence, St. Joseph is one of the great patrons of the contemplative life. A contemplative life is characterized by a certain hiddenness, silence, and interior communion with God. In the Church, there are religious orders that are contemplative such as the Carmelites, Trappists, and the Carthusians. These consecrated men and women model something to which we are all called. Every Christian's life should have a

· ·

35   *Pope Benedict XVI, Angelus, December 18, 2005. Spiritual Thoughts in the First Year of his Papacy, Libreria Editrice Vaticana, p. 77*

contemplative dimension. The contemplative spirit of St. Joseph was lived in a particular way during the "hidden years" of Nazareth. Jesus, Mary, and Joseph lived a simple and ordinary family life while continuously adoring God. Contemplatives understand St. Joseph and consider him one of them. There are many things contemplatives have in common with St. Joseph.

One of the characteristics of the contemplative life is silence. Silence is a beautiful thing for those who are able to enter into its mystery. Silence should not be seen as the absence of something, but rather a posture of openness and receptivity to the Divine Presence. A contemplative is someone who is at home in silence. Sacred silence is one of the delights of the contemplative life. In all of Scripture, St. Joseph does not say a single word. He was a man of silence.

Another characteristic of contemplatives is that they do not seek worldly attention. Joseph, though he was a great man, lived a humble life. He did not win any great military battles, take on false prophets, or convert the masses. He worked as a carpenter and was a faithful family man. Joseph lived a hidden life. Contemplatives do not seek human esteem but rather the favor of God.

Work is also an essential part of a contemplative's life. St. Joseph's days were spent working as a carpenter. God could have chosen a wealthy man with many servants to be His Son's earthly father, but instead He chose a humble tradesman who had calluses on his hands. A contemplative's day is filled with work. We are meant to enjoy leisure but not to be idle. Our time should be spent purposely even when resting or relaxing.

As a consequence of the Fall, Adam had to work by the sweat of his brow.[36] Every punishment of God is remedial; it is always a medicine that heals. Work is meant to restore our souls. In order for work to be good and healing, it must be given its proper place. This is something contemplatives model for us. Contemplatives always work at a leisurely pace. They don't have the frantic busyness that is so common in the work

. . . .

36   Gen 3:19

30

world. Ambitiously trying to climb the ladder and to achieve at all costs has no place in the contemplative life. Contemplatives always work with a certain interior peace and detachment that allows them to keep their hearts fixed on God.

Contemplatives live a life of simplicity. Joseph's family was free from worldly riches. As a carpenter, Joseph was able to provide for his family. He didn't live the grinding poverty we see in some parts of the world that is often a result of injustice. Joseph lived the simple life of a rural carpenter. All his basic needs were met and he did not want anything more. Rather than focusing on the things of the world, he focused his life on the true treasures in his home: Jesus and Mary. The family of Nazareth was detached from worldly riches. Their hearts were fixed on the things of Heaven, where our true and lasting treasure is found.

One way Joseph expressed his love to Our Lady was by honoring her total consecration to God. The Church teaches that Mary is the Perpetual Virgin; she is virgin before, during and after birth. Though Joseph had Mary as his wife, he lived a life of sexual continence with her.

Marriage and sexual union are part of God's plan for humanity. His first commandment was *"Be fruitful and multiply."*[37] Sexuality is a gift from God and a great good. However, St. Joseph recognized that honoring Mary's total consecration to God through sexual continence was an even greater good.

Similarly, those who live a consecrated life forsake the good of sexual intimacy for *"the sake of the kingdom of Heaven."*[38] For example, the Catechism states that consecrated women are *"called by the Lord to cling only to Him with greater freedom of heart, body, and spirit."*[39] Each one of us is called to live chastity according to his or her state in life. While that call may take different forms, it always requires some degree of self-sacrifice, which St. Joseph models for us.

. . . .

37   *Genesis 1:28*
38   *Matthew 19:12*
39   *Catechism of the Catholic Church paragraph 922*

Another mark of the contemplative life is what the early church fathers called the "sober intoxication of the Spirit." The contemplative drinks deeply from the living waters, which Jesus promised to give us. *"The water I shall give will become in him a spring of water welling up to eternal life.*"[40] There is a sublime delight, an intoxication that comes with emptying oneself so as to be filled with God. Joseph is a model of total self-emptying. He did not live for himself. His life was totally given over to the will of God, which was to serve Jesus and Mary. Joy is a supernatural gift from God. The way to open the floodgates of joy in our lives is to do the will of God. As our lives are given over to God's will, a mysterious flow begins to course through the depths of our beings. This is God's Spirit living and moving in us. The life of Nazareth, though simple and silent, would have been one of sublime delight. Mary and Joseph could have said with the psalmist: My cup overflows.[41]

St. Joseph, model of contemplatives, pray for us!

Memorare to St. Joseph

Remember, O most chaste spouse of the Virgin Mary, that never was it known that anyone who implored your help and sought your intercession were left unassisted.
Full of confidence in your power I fly unto you and beg your protection. Despise not O Guardian of the Redeemer my humble supplication, but in your bounty, hear and answer me. Amen.

Our Father, Hail Mary, Glory be...

. . . .
40   *John 4:14*
41   *Psalm 23:5*

DAY 5
St. Joseph and the Patriarch Joseph

Go to Joseph! – St. Brother Andre (*see Genesis 41:55*)

The patriarch Joseph in many ways prefigures St. Joseph, the foster father of Jesus.[42] It is not likely a coincidence that these two men share the same name. In this chapter, we will look at the story of the patriarch Joseph and highlight some of the parallels between these two great men.

The Patriarch Joseph was the eleventh of the twelve sons of Jacob. Jacob was the son of Isaac, who was the son of Abraham. Scripture also refers to Jacob as Israel because God changed Jacob's name to Israel. *"And God said to him, 'Your name is Jacob; no longer shall your name be called Jacob, but Israel shall be your name.'"*[43]

Joseph was his father's favorite son, which caused envy among his brothers. *"Now Israel loved Joseph more than any other of his children, because he was the son of his old age; and he made him a long robe with sleeves. But when his brothers saw that their father loved him more than all his brothers, they hated him, and could not speak peaceably to him."*[44]

. . . .

42   *The patriarch Joseph is primarily a prefiguring of the Lord Jesus,*
      which is a fascinating study beyond the scope of this book.
43   *Genesis 35:10*
44   *Genesis 37:3-4*

The patriarch Joseph was a dreamer. One day, he had a dream that he shared with his brothers. *"He said to them, 'Hear this dream which I have dreamed: behold, we were binding sheaves in the field, and lo, my sheaf arose and stood upright; and behold, your sheaves gathered round it, and bowed down to my sheaf.'"* [45] The brothers were not impressed by this dream and asked Joseph if he thought he would reign over them. This seemed to be the obvious meaning of his dream.

Then Joseph had another dream. *"'Behold, I have dreamed another dream; and behold, the sun, the moon, and eleven stars were bowing down to me.'"* [46] This too, the brothers were not impressed with. Even Joseph's father rebuked him, saying: *"'What is this dream that you have dreamed? Shall I and your mother and your brothers indeed come to bow ourselves to the ground before you?'"* [47]

The patriarch Joseph had dreams that disturbed his father and brothers, but were nevertheless from God. So too, St. Joseph was gifted with heavenly dreams that helped direct his life according to God's purposes. It was through dreams that Joseph was asked to take Mary as his wife, to flee to Egypt, and later to return to Israel. Both Josephs were dreamers!

The story of our patriarch continues. One day Israel sent Joseph to see his brothers who were pasturing the flock in Shechem. As Joseph was approaching them, they saw him and said to one another: *"'Here comes this dreamer. Come now, let us kill him and throw him into one of the pits; then we shall say that a wild beast has devoured him, and we shall see what will become of his dreams.'"* [48] But then they saw some traders passing by on their way to Egypt and decided to sell him to the traders instead. They sold Joseph to the Egyptian traders for twenty shekels of silver. Thus, another parallel exists between St. Joseph and the patriarch Joseph is that they were both exiled to Egypt. Centuries after the patriarch was sold to Egyptian slave traders, St. Joseph had to flee to Egypt to escape

. . . .

45   *Genesis 37:6-7*
46   *Genesis 37:9*
47   *Genesis 37:10*
48   *Genesis 37:19-20*

Herod who was trying to kill Jesus.

In Egypt, our patriarch Joseph is sold to an Egyptian as a slave. The Egyptian immediately notices that Joseph is a very responsible and trustworthy man. *"His master saw that the LORD was with him, and that the LORD caused all that he did to prosper in his hands. So Joseph found favor in his sight and attended him, and he made him overseer of his house and put him in charge of all that he had. So he left all that he had in Joseph's charge; and having him he had no concern for anything but the food which he ate.*[49] Joseph carried out his duties so well that his Egyptian master put him in charge of everything he had.

Things were going well, but Scripture goes on to say: *"Now Joseph was handsome and good looking. And after a time his master's wife cast her eyes upon Joseph, and said, 'Lie with me.'"*[50] Joseph's master's wife was attracted to Joseph and tried to seduce him. However, Joseph was a righteous man who feared God and refused her seductions. He responded to her, *"'How then could I do this great wrong and sin against God?'"*[51] Finally she tried to force herself upon him and he ran away, but she held on to his cloak and yelled. She lied and claimed that Joseph was trying to force himself upon her. Joseph was immediately thrown in prison. Through this trial, the patriarch Joseph demonstrated great integrity, purity, and an unwillingness to offend God. Similarly, St. Joseph models purity in his chaste love for the Ever-Virgin Mary. Both of these great men stand out as remarkable models of unfaltering virtue.

In prison, Joseph's gifts once again became apparent. Scripture tells us, *"The keeper of the prison committed to Joseph's care all the prisoners who were in the prison and whatever was done there, he was the doer of it; the keeper of the prison paid no heed to anything that was in Joseph's care, because the LORD was with him; and whatever he did, the LORD made it prosper."*[52] For a second time, Joseph is put in charge of everything.

. . . .

49   *Genesis 39:3-6*
50   *Genesis 39:6-7*
51   *Genesis 39:9 (NAB)*
52   *Genesis 39:22-23*

Pharaoh was upset with his butler and baker and sends them to prison. In prison, Joseph noticed they were upset and asked them what was wrong. They told him that they had had dreams and didn't know how to interpret them. Joseph interprets their dreams for them. He says to the butler that in three days he would be pouring Pharaoh's wine again, but he says to the baker that in three days he would be killed by Pharaoh. As predicted, in three days the butler was back in Pharaoh's service pouring his wine, but the baker was hanged by Pharaoh. Joseph asked the butler to remember him when he was back in Pharaoh's service and to help get him out of prison.

The butler forgot about Joseph until two years later when Pharaoh had a dream about seven fat cows and seven skinny cows. When no one was able to interpret Pharaoh's dream, the butler remembered Joseph. He told Pharaoh about Joseph, and Pharaoh called for him. Joseph said Pharaoh's dream foretold a coming famine. Seven years of plenty would be followed by seven years of famine. Joseph recommended what should be done in preparation. *"So Pharaoh said to Joseph, 'Since God has shown you all this, there is none so discreet and wise as you are; you shall be over my house, and all my people shall order themselves as you command; only as regards the throne will I be greater than you.'"*[53] For the third time, Joseph was put in charge of a household, this time the whole kingdom.

Three times, Joseph rose from utter destitution to being the number one person in charge. He moved from slavery to being the head of a household, from imprisonment to managing a prison, and again from imprisonment to having charge of a kingdom. Staggering! Clearly, the Lord was with Joseph.

Just as the patriarch Joseph always found himself in charge of a household, so too St. Joseph found himself in charge of a household: the Lord's household. In the litany of St. Joseph, we invoke Joseph as head of the Holy Family. Also, in the liturgy of the Church on the feast of St. Joseph, the Preface gives thanks to God for giving St. Joseph *"as a wise*

53   *Genesis 41:39-40*

and faithful servant in charge of your household."[54] God entrusted Jesus His Beloved Son and Mary the Blessed Virgin to Joseph, knowing that in his care all would be well. The Son would be protected, provided for, sheltered, properly educated, and properly nurtured.

Because Joseph properly interpreted Pharaoh's dream, the kingdom was prepared for the coming famine. As food ran out, the people of the surrounding nations came to Egypt hoping to receive the bread that Joseph distributed. One day, Joseph's brothers came and knelt before him, looking for bread. Scripture tells us, "*When Joseph recognized his brothers, although they did not recognize him, he was reminded of the dreams he had about them.*"[55] Joseph gives them bread, reveals himself to them and forgives them. By providing bread for his brothers, Joseph saved the lives of his family. Just as the patriarch Joseph was the one who provided bread, so too St. Joseph was the man chosen to provide bread for Jesus, the Son of God. The humble carpenter of Nazareth had the privilege of nourishing the One who would one day proclaim: "*I am the living bread which came down from heaven.*"[56]

Finally, Scripture makes no mention of the patriarch Joseph committing any faults. He is portrayed as a truly righteous man. Likewise, in the Gospels, St. Joseph is the faithful foster father of Jesus. He is the man who selflessly obeys every one of God's commands. God the Father chose a perfect woman to be mother of Jesus and also chose a holy and faithful man to be His father. We are reminded of St. Joseph when we hear Our Lord saying: "*Who then is the faithful and wise steward, whom his master will set over his household, to give them their portion of food at the proper time? Blessed is that servant whom his master when he comes will find so doing. Truly, I say to you, he will set him over all his possessions.*[57]"

St. Joseph, Splendor of Patriarchs, pray for us!

. . . .

54   *Preface, Feast of St. Joseph, March 19th*
55   *Genesis 42:8-9a (NAB)*
56   *John 6:51*
57   *Luke 12:42-44*

Memorare to St. Joseph

Remember, O most chaste spouse of the Virgin Mary, that never was it known that anyone who implored your help and sought your intercession were left unassisted.
Full of confidence in your power I fly unto you and beg your protection. Despise not O Guardian of the Redeemer my humble supplication, but in your bounty, hear and answer me. Amen.

Our Father, Hail Mary, Glory be...

DAY 6
Glory of Home Life

───────────── ✦ ─────────────

*I love St. Joseph so much "because he had the
care of the Blessed Virgin".*[58] - St. John Vianney

One of the things that make it easy to identify with St. Joseph is the fact
that he was a family man. In the litany to St. Joseph, we invoke him as
Head of the Holy Family, Spouse of the Mother of God, Glory of Home
Life, and Pillar of Families.

Joseph was married to the Blessed Virgin Mary. As Catholics, we
understand the importance of having a devotion to Our Lady. After Jesus,
there is no one who was more devoted to Mary than her husband, Joseph.
Imagine the love that Joseph had for his wife. Think about how well he
knew the Blessed Virgin Mary. He is the one who cared and provided
for her. Our Lady is the Immaculate Conception. She was conceived
without sin. She is in a category of her own. However, in marriage there
is a sharing of goods. Spouses share material goods, spiritual goods, and
ultimately the gift of themselves. Joseph and Mary would have been,
to a degree, compatible even spiritually. They walked together in faith.
Joseph's family was indeed a holy family.

. . . .

58   *Saint John Vianney, Notre-Dame d'Ars, Meditation 6; Tan, Thoughts
         of the Curé d'Ars*

As husband and wife, Mary and Joseph provided the sacred home life of Nazareth, the first and most perfect Christian community. Though hidden, the life of the Holy Family has always been a model and inspiration for Christians. Let us ponder what this Holy Family would have been like.

The family of Nazareth would have been a place of great love. God is love. Because Jesus is God made man, His most Sacred Heart is a heart burning with infinite love. The heart of Jesus is an inexhaustible fountain of love, an ocean of love. Love wants to give of itself. Can you imagine the love Jesus would have poured out into that home? How blessed were Mary and Joseph to be the direct recipients of the love of Jesus! Joseph not only shared life with the Lord of Love but also with Our Blessed Mother. The Immaculate Heart of Mary was totally united to God. Her heart, too, was overflowing with love. Joseph would have shared in this communion of love. It is said that the love among Jesus, Mary and Joseph was an earthly reflection of the Holy Trinity. The great love in this home was the closest thing to Heaven on Earth.

Jesus loved people with a beautiful tenderness. He was a man who was not afraid to show affection. Sometimes we stereotype religious people as being cold, inhibited, stern, stoic and stiff. Jesus was not any of those things. He was a man who touched people, even sinners. He loved to draw the children to himself so He could bless them. He shared meals with people and enjoyed their company. People were drawn to him. He was also a man who wept; he was not afraid to show emotion. Our Lord was an affectionate man. Therefore, when we think about how Jesus, Mary, and Joseph would have interacted with each other, we can imagine that it would have been with great tenderness. Not only was Nazareth a place of love, it was a place of tender and affectionate love.

The home of Nazareth also would have been a place of prayer and studying Scripture. We know that Jesus was literate; he was able to read and write. The Gospel of Luke tells us that Jesus read in the synagogue, as was his custom.[59] There's no question that Jesus knew the scriptures. Faithful Jews were devoted to learning, studying, memorizing, and pondering

. . . .

59   *Luke 4:16*

40

Scripture continually. Psalm 1 states, *"Blessed is the man who walks not in the counsel of the wicked, nor stands in the way of sinners, nor sits in the seat of scoffers; but his delight is in the law of the LORD, and on his law he meditates day and night.*[60]*"* The Church Fathers taught that this Psalm refers primarily to the Lord Jesus. He is the blessed man who pondered God's law day and night. The home of Nazareth was a place of prayerfully studying God's law.

However, that doesn't mean that the family life of Nazareth was always serious and solemn. Many of us would be tempted to see the Holy Family's life as dull and boring, imagining them always in formal prayer, practicing pious devotions, and oblivious to the world around them. But this is not the case. Have you ever noticed that when you meet a saintly person he is always interesting, creative, and never predictable? In the lives of the saints, we find a creativity and a uniqueness that is rarely found in worldly people. Jesus said, *"I came that they may have life, and have it abundantly."*[61] There would have been an abundance of life in the home of Nazareth.

The home of Nazareth was also a place of joy. Life is ultimately a gift from God. As children of God, we are called to live under God's blessing and to recognize that we are fundamentally blessed. We have reason to rejoice. The Psalmist proclaims, *"This is the day which the LORD has made; let us rejoice and be glad in it.*[62]*"* The family of Nazareth would have been a place where the simplicity of ordinary life was enjoyed. They would have been able to enjoy the gift of the present moment. They would have served the Lord with gladness.

Family life is meant to be enjoyed. Jesus, Mary and Joseph reflected the mutual self-giving love of the Blessed Trinity. Our families too should be a little foretaste of Heaven. Our families should be places where we pour ourselves out in love for one another. Family life can often times be a struggle, but if we persevere in seeking God and being faithful to him, we

. . . .

60   *Psalm 1:1-2*
61   *John 10:10*
62   *Psalm 118:24*

41

will find family life satisfying.

A satisfying life is found in faithfulness to one's duty and one's vocation. Unfortunately, many people see family life as a burden. Rather, family life, properly embraced, is a great source of life. God made it that way. A real man, a man of God, finds family life satisfying. St. Joseph is the Glory of Home Life and the Pillar of Families. God chose him to model manhood, fatherhood, and family life to His Son, and he also models it for us. Let's ask him to pray for us that we too may find delight in family life.

St. Joseph, Mainstay of Families, pray for us!

Memorare to St. Joseph

Remember, O most chaste spouse of the Virgin Mary, that never was it known that anyone who implored your help and sought your intercession were left unassisted.
Full of confidence in your power I fly unto you and beg your protection. Despise not O Guardian of the Redeemer my humble supplication, but in your bounty, hear and answer me. Amen.

Our Father, Hail Mary, Glory be...

DAY 7
Diligent Protector of Christ

———— ✍ ————

St. Joseph was a just man, a tireless worker, the upright guardian of those entrusted to his care. May he always guard, protect and enlighten families. - Pope St. John Paul II

Today, let us look at the story of the flight to Egypt and the qualities of Joseph that it reveals to us. We will also reflect on some of Joseph's titles: Diligent Protector of Christ, Joseph Most Obedient, Terror of Demons, and Protector of Holy Church.

Jesus was born during the reign of King Herod. As Matthew's Gospel tells us, three wise men saw a star and came to Jerusalem inquiring about the birthplace of *"the newborn king of the Jews."*[63] They were told he was to be born in Bethlehem. Herod *"sent them to Bethlehem and said, 'Go and search diligently for the child. When you have found him, bring me word, that I too may go and do him homage.'"*[64] In reality, however, Herod felt threatened at the possibility of a new king and was planning to have him killed. The wise men found Jesus in Bethlehem, paid him homage, and gave him gifts. But *"having been warned in a dream not to return to Herod, they departed for their country by another way."*[65]

. . . .

63   *Matthew 2:2*
64   *Matthew 2:8*
65   *Matthew 2:12*

Because Joseph was attentive and obedient to God's will, he was able to protect and guard the infant Jesus from the threat of Herod. *"When the three wisemen had departed from Bethlehem, behold an angel of the Lord appeared to Joseph in a dream and said, "Rise, take the child and his mother and flee to Egypt and remain there until I tell you; for Herod is about to search for the child to destroy him." And he rose and took the child and his mother by night and departed to Egypt and remained there until the death of Herod. [...] Then Herod when he saw that he had been tricked by the wise men, was in a furious rage and he sent and killed all the male children in Bethlehem and in all that region who were two years old and under."*[66]

The first quality of St. Joseph that we notice is his attentiveness to God's will. Though he heard from the Lord in his sleep, Joseph was always spiritually awake. He was like a watchman. A constant danger in the spiritual life is to become so caught up in the vanities and noise of this world that we lose our ability to hear God's still small voice guiding us. When the angel of the Lord spoke to Joseph in a dream, he recognized God's voice. He didn't miss it. We can think of Joseph when we hear Our Lord's words, *"Blessed are those servants whom the master finds awake when he comes."*[67] Joseph is one of the blessed servants of God.

It is very interesting that the Lord chose to give these directions to Joseph rather than Mary. We know that the Blessed Virgin Mary was the most spiritually docile woman who has ever lived. Yet when God chose to communicate these directions, he communicated them to Joseph. This confirms that in a marriage covenant, husband and wife enter into a partnership. Even though Joseph was married to the holiest of women, God honored Joseph's shared dignity and responsibility. St. Joseph did not abdicate his responsibility as father of the family. Instead, he accepted and embraced this role. Our Lady knew that her husband, Joseph was hearing God's word clearly. She trusted him enough to leave the country in the middle of the night, fleeing the powers of darkness that were trying to kill the child.

. . . .

66   *Matthew 2:13-16*
67   *Luke 12:37*

44

At a time when his family was in danger, Joseph once again proved his immediate and perfect obedience. Even when God asked Joseph to do unexpected and difficult things, the humble carpenter simply obeyed. Joseph did not question, nor did he try to discuss terms and conditions. We see this consistently with St. Joseph, which earns him the title "Joseph Most Obedient." The humble carpenter demonstrated an obedience that is almost unparalleled in all of Scripture.

In the Litany, we also invoke Joseph as Protector of Holy Church. By guarding his son against the rage of Herod, the Foster Father of Jesus was already protecting the Church in seminal form. The Church is the Body of Christ. Not only did Joseph literally protect the Body of Christ in Jesus' childhood, he continues to protect the mystical Body of Christ, the Church. Many times when the Catholic Church has been under attack by dangerous ideologies and political movements, popes have turned to St. Joseph, asking for his special protection and intercession. In the book of Revelation, John describes the Woman, who symbolizes the Church.[68] This Woman battles with the Red Dragon, who wants to devour her child. By fleeing to Egypt with Mary and Jesus, Joseph protected the Woman and the Child.

It was not only Herod who was trying to destroy the newborn Savior, but all the powers of darkness. Jesus was under attack by both worldly and spiritual forces. Joseph's mission was to protect Jesus from those forces. God gave him the grace to do so. Catholic theology calls this "grace of state." Grace of state means that God always provides the graces necessary to carry out God's will, especially relating to one's vocation. Parents are responsible for the temporal and spiritual welfare of their children. Therefore, fathers and mothers are given authority to bless and to bind. If there are powers of darkness directed against a family the parents have the authority to bind those powers and to command them to be gone. Imagine all the powers of hell directed against the Savior, the Lamb of God who has come to take away the sins of the world. According to God's divine order, Joseph as father, had authority to command those powers to flee. Thus,

. . . .

68   *Revelation 12:3-4*

45

another one of Joseph's titles is Terror of Demons.

The story of the flight to Egypt highlights how the Foster Father of Jesus diligently protected his child. We see in St. Joseph a man who was attentive to God's voice and the promptings of the Spirit. We see a man who was obedient to God and assumed his role as protector of his family. Joseph was a man who knew his authority over the powers of darkness directed against Jesus and Mary. He was the exemplary guardian of the Holy Family and wants to be a loving guardian for each of us as well.

St. Joseph, Watchful Defender of Christ, pray for us!

Memorare to St. Joseph

Remember, O most chaste spouse of the Virgin Mary, that never was it known that anyone who implored your help and sought your intercession were left unassisted.
Full of confidence in your power I fly unto you and beg your protection. Despise not O Guardian of the Redeemer my humble supplication, but in your bounty, hear and answer me. Amen.

Our Father, Hail Mary, Glory be...

DAY 8
Patron of a Happy Death

———— ⌒✦⌒ ————

I do not remember that I ever asked St. Joseph
at any time for anything which he did not obtain
for me. [69]- St. Theresa of Avila

In the Litany of St. Joseph, we invoke St. Joseph as "Patron of the Dying." It is a pious tradition that Joseph died in the arms of Jesus and Mary. This is why we consider Joseph the patron of a happy death and ask him to pray for us that we too may die a happy death. It is good and beneficial for us to meditate on our passing from this life to the next. In the book of Sirach we are told, *"In all you do, remember the end of your life, and then you will never sin."* [70] St. Joseph gives us hope as we contemplate the reality that one day we too will be called to our eternal home.

It is likely that Joseph died before Jesus began his public ministry. There are two things in Scripture that seem to indicate this. First, Joseph's presence is never mentioned during Jesus' public ministry. By contrast, Scripture tells us that Our Lady was with Jesus during those three years. A second hint that Joseph would have died before Jesus began his public ministry is that Jesus left Nazareth. Matthew tells us, *"He left Nazareth and went to live in Capernaum by the sea.*[71]*"* Jesus grew up in Nazareth

. . . .

69   *St. Teresa of Avila, Autobiography, Chapter XI*
70   *Sirach 7:36*
71   *Matthew 4:13*

and worked as a carpenter with Joseph. In Jesus' time, it was typical for a son to learn his father's trade and to work and live with his father until his father's death. Once the father had died, the son could go off and establish himself somewhere else. So Jesus' moving to Capernaum could indicate that Joseph had passed away.

We can understand why it could have been necessary for Joseph to pass on before Jesus began his public ministry. Joseph's role and mission was to protect the child. Already in Jesus' infancy, Joseph protected Jesus and kept him hidden from Herod, who tried to kill Him. Had Joseph been alive when Jesus was condemned to death, Joseph would have died protecting his son. However, Jesus was born to die. Jesus is the Lamb of God who came to take away the sins of the world. He had to lay down his life in sacrifice for us. Joseph's mission was to protect the Lamb until His time came. Perhaps in God's providential plan, Joseph the protector was called home so that the Savior could fulfill his mission.

If Joseph did die before Jesus began his public ministry, it is likely that the pious tradition that he died in the arms of Jesus and Mary is accurate. We know that Jesus was close to his family. He lived in Nazareth with Mary until he began his public ministry. It only makes sense that Jesus would have wanted to be present when His foster father died, just as any loving son would. Mary, too, would have been with her devoted husband in his last moments. There's no better way to die than in the arms of Jesus and Mary.

Joseph died with the grace of having fulfilled his mission. His mission was to be a father to the Son of God, to care for Jesus as his own son. St. Joseph could have said with St. Paul, *"I have competed well; I have finished the race; I have kept the faith. From now on the crown of righteousness awaits me, which the Lord, the just judge, will award to me..."*[72] Is this not what we all hope to say one day as the Lord is calling us home?

We can only imagine the last moments of Joseph's life. Joseph, who was led by God his whole life, would have abandoned himself to God even in

---

[72]   *2 Timothy 4:7-8*

death. We know that Joseph was a man of few words. Perhaps he simply gazed deeply into the eyes of Our Lord and Our Blessed Mother as tears rolled down their cheeks. Jesus would have shown great love and affection to the man who cared for Him as a child. Jesus and Joseph had spent so many years working side by side in the carpentry shop and on the work site. Jesus was not only losing his earthly father and his workmate, but perhaps also his closest friend. It has often been said that Joseph was the man closest to Jesus. We can imagine the grief in Our Lord's Heart as He said goodbye to the man with whom He had become so close. Jesus would have entrusted his foster father to His Father in Heaven. Mary too would have expressed her tender love to the man who was so devoted to her and with whom she shared such a remarkable life. She would have entrusted to God her husband whom she loved so dearly. Mary too would have been filled with sorrow as she said goodbye to her faithful and loving husband yet, even in the sorrow, there would have been deep faith and confidence in God. Joseph's passing must have been filled with profound spiritual consolation and joy. He died a happy death.

Contemplating Joseph's holy death is meant to help us prepare for our own death. It is good to surrender to the Lord when and how we will die, trusting in His holy and perfect will. We can pray that our passing is filled with peace and joy; that the Lord protect us from all fear and despair. As Christians, we should all pray for the grace of final perseverance, that we might be faithful to the Lord until our dying breath. We can ask that we die having received the last sacraments. We pray that our hearts be filled with the love of God as we pass on to eternal life. Above all, we should ask God that we die in a state of grace. All of us should pray to God that, like St. Joseph, we might die a holy and happy death.

Joseph models for us how to live and how to die. He died a happy death. He left this world having fulfilled his mission. We ask St. Joseph to pray for us that we too may live well and die well.

St. Joseph, Patron of the Dying, pray for us!

Memorare to St. Joseph

Remember, O most chaste spouse of the Virgin Mary, that never was it known that anyone who implored your help and sought your intercession were left unassisted.
Full of confidence in your power I fly unto you and beg your protection. Despise not O Guardian of the Redeemer my humble supplication, but in your bounty, hear and answer me. Amen.

Our Father, Hail Mary, Glory be...

DAY 9
Universal Patron

―――――⁓⧸―――――

The example of St. Joseph, a "just man," the Evangelist says, fully responsible before God and before Mary, should be an encouragement to all of you on your way towards the priesthood... I can assure you, dear seminarians, that the further you advance with God's grace on the path of the priesthood, the more you will experience what abundant spiritual fruits result from calling on St. Joseph and invoking his support in carrying out your daily duty[73]. - Pope Benedict XVI

Today, on the last day of our preparation for entrustment, we look to St. Joseph as universal patron. The Church invites all people to have a devotion to the foster father of Jesus. St. Joseph is for everyone. We can all find something St. Joseph models that inspires us. Let us look at some of the areas that fall under this great saint's patronage.

Joseph was the foster father of Jesus and is therefore the patron of fathers. All fatherhood is meant to image the Fatherhood of God. Joseph is the man who most perfectly reflected God in his fatherhood. One of the ways Our Lord honored and obeyed His Heavenly Father was by honoring and obeying his earthly father. Men who have been given the dignity and

· ·

73   *Pope Benedict XVI, Address to the Roman Major Seminary, February 25, 2006. Spiritual Thoughts in the First Year of his Papacy. Libreria Editrice Vaticana, p. 105.*

responsibility of fatherhood can ask Joseph to help them be good fathers.

Joseph is also the patron of husbands. He was the husband of the Immaculate Virgin. A total and radical self-emptying marked Joseph's vocation. Married men can learn how to respect their wives from Joseph, who selflessly guarded Our Blessed Mother's purity. Ladies can entrust themselves to St. Joseph, who cares for his spiritual daughters with a pure and manly love. It is good for young people to entrust themselves to Joseph, Guardian of Virgins. Joseph is well known for helping young people guard their innocence.

With Our Lady, Joseph is the patron of the family. Every family should be entrusted to the Holy Family. Joseph is a model of manhood. Men should draw inspiration from Joseph, the Just Man. Many people, especially those lacking proper fathering, have experienced Joseph's paternal love by entrusting themselves to this humble carpenter.

St. Joseph is the patron of workers. He was a worker, and had to work to provide for his family. He is also a patron of the poor. Since St. Joseph also experienced poverty, especially when Jesus was born, he is the help of those who turn to him when times are hard. However, he is also a patron of the rich. The rich can identify with Joseph because as a son of David, he was of royal descent. Joseph also had the two greatest treasures in his home: Jesus and Mary. Joseph helps the rich remember that our real treasure is in Heaven.

Joseph has the title "Solace of the wretched." During his flight to Egypt, Joseph had to leave his homeland in the middle of the night with his family and only a few possessions. This would have surely been a great hardship for Joseph. He had to find work in a strange land, possibly without speaking the language or knowing anyone. For this reason, St. Joseph is also the patron of those looking for work. People who are struggling in life can turn to Joseph to find someone who understands their situation. Those who are away from their home country and new immigrants can also turn to Joseph because he empathizes with the struggles of living in a foreign land. Joseph can help us when life becomes difficult.

Clergy can also take Joseph as a patron. Bishops, priests and deacons are custodians of the mysteries of God and most importantly custodians of Jesus in the Blessed Sacrament. St. Joseph was guardian of the Lord Jesus during his earthly life, so clergy look to him for help with this great responsibility. Furthermore, St. Joseph is a fitting patron of the clergy because he is also the patron of contemplatives and those who live a consecrated life.

These are only a few examples of those who can come under St. Joseph's patronage, though anyone can find devotion to him beneficial. He is a universal patron.

* * *

Why are so many people, from all walks of life, drawn to Joseph? Here are three reasons this silent man is so widely loved. First, he models 'being' rather than 'doing.' What we do is important, but it's not nearly as important as who we are, our character. In the world's eyes, this humble carpenter did nothing great, but in God's eyes, this carpenter faithfully carried out one of the most important missions a human being could be given. Joseph was a just man, a quality worth more than any worldly accomplishment. We love Joseph because he reminds us about what is most important.

The second reason why devotion to St. Joseph is so popular is that he models sanctity in the ordinary life. He was a carpenter, a husband, and a family man living a hidden life. Though he was an ordinary man, he lived an ordinary life in an extraordinary way. Almost all of us can identify with how common Joseph's life was. When we look at saints like John the Baptist, who lived an austere life of penance, or Peter, who was called to walk with Jesus for three years and lead the church, or Paul, who undertook great missionary journeys, we might feel that holiness is not for us. A truck driver, however, can identify with Joseph. A mother, who cares for her family, can identify with Joseph. We can all identify with Joseph. That's why we love him so much.

The final characteristic that draws us to St. Joseph is his humility. Even common wisdom states that humility is attractive. Joseph's humility is one of his most prominent features. Joseph was a great man who was never looking for attention. We are all drawn to such humility.

St. Joseph is a model for all Christians. The Church invites us to find a friend in St. Joseph. Let us entrust ourselves to the foster father of Jesus. With Our Lord and Our Blessed Mother, let us allow Joseph to be our guardian and protector.

St. Joseph, Protector of the Holy Church, pray for us!

Memorare to St. Joseph

Remember, O most chaste spouse of the Virgin Mary, that never was it known that anyone who implored your help and sought your intercession were left unassisted.
Full of confidence in your power I fly unto you and beg your protection. Despise not O Guardian of the Redeemer my humble supplication, but in your bounty, hear and answer me. Amen.

Our Father, Hail Mary, Glory Be...

Entrustment Prayer

Dear St. Joseph, I entrust myself today to your loving care.

Be my protector and guide on this earthly pilgrimage.

Intercede for me that, like you,

I may be truly devoted to Jesus and Mary.

Amen.

Feasts of St. Joseph

Holy Family – Sunday within the Octave of Christmas, or, if there is no Sunday, December 30*

March 19 – Solemnity of St. Joseph

May 1st – St. Joseph the Worker

Feast	Start Day	Feast Day (Entrustment Day)
Holy Family	9 days before the Feast	Sunday after Christmas*
Solemnity of St. Joseph	March 11	March 19
St. Joseph the Worker	April 23	May 1

Litany of St. Joseph

Lord, have mercy.

Lord, have mercy.

Christ, have mercy.

Christ, have mercy.

Lord, have mercy.

Lord, have mercy.

Jesus, hear us.

Jesus, graciously hear us.

God, the Father of Heaven,

have mercy on us.

God, the Son, Redeemer of the world,

have mercy on us.

God, the Holy Spirit,

have mercy on us.

Holy Trinity, One God,

have mercy on us.

Holy Mary,

pray for us.

St. Joseph,

pray for us.

Renowned offspring of David,

pray for us.

Light of Patriarchs,

pray for us.

Spouse of the Mother of God,

pray for us.

Chaste guardian of the Virgin,

pray for us.

Foster father of the Son of God,	*pray for us.*
Diligent protector of Christ,	*pray for us.*
Head of the Holy Family,	*pray for us.*
Joseph most just,	*pray for us.*
Joseph most chaste,	*pray for us.*
Joseph most prudent,	*pray for us.*
Joseph most strong,	*pray for us.*
Joseph most obedient,	*pray for us.*
Joseph most faithful,	*pray for us.*
Mirror of patience,	*pray for us.*
Lover of poverty,	*pray for us.*
Model of workers,	*pray for us.*
Glory of home life,	*pray for us.*
Guardian of virgins,	*pray for us.*
Pillar of families,	*pray for us.*
Solace of the wretched,	*pray for us.*
Hope of the sick,	*pray for us.*
Patron of the dying,	*pray for us.*
Terror of demons,	*pray for us.*
Protector of Holy Church,	*pray for us.*

Lamb of God, who take away the sins of the world,   *spare us, O Lord.*

Lamb of God, who take away the sins of the world,   *graciously hear us, O Lord.*

Lamb of God, who take away the sins of the world.   *Have mercy on us.*

He made him the lord of His household.   *And prince over all His possessions.*

Let us pray, O God, in Your ineffable providence You were pleased to choose Blessed Joseph to be the spouse of your most holy Mother; grant, we beg, that we may be worthy to have him for our intercessor in heaven whom on earth we venerate as our Protector: You who live and reign forever and ever.

Other Prayers to St. Joseph

PRAYER FOR PURITY

St. Joseph, father and guardian of virgins, into whose faithful keeping were entrusted innocence itself, Christ Jesus, and Mary, the Virgin of virgins, I pray and beseech you through Jesus and Mary, those pledges so dear to you, to keep me from all uncleanness, and to grant that my mind may be untainted, my heart pure, and my body chaste; help me always to serve Jesus and Mary in perfect chastity. *Amen.*

PROTECTION PRAYER

Oh, St. Joseph, whose protection is so great, so strong, so prompt before the throne of God, I place in you all my interests and desires. Oh, St. Joseph, do assist me by your powerful intercession, and obtain for me from your divine Son all spiritual blessings, through Jesus Christ, our Lord. So that, having engaged here below your heavenly power, I may offer my thanksgiving and homage to the most loving of fathers.

Oh, St. Joseph, I never weary contemplating you, and Jesus asleep in your arms; I dare not approach while He reposes near your heart. Press Him in my name and kiss His fine head for me and ask Him to return the kiss when I draw my dying breath. St. Joseph, patron of departing souls – Pray for me.

About the Author

Fr. Mark Goring is a member of the Companions of the Cross, a new order of priests based in Ottawa, Ontario. He grew up in the town of Pembroke, in the Ottawa valley. He joined the Companions of the Cross when he was 18 and was ordained to the priesthood in 2002, at the age of 26. Fr. Mark is the Assistant General Superior of the Companions of the Cross. He is the Director of the Catholic Charismatic Center in Houston, Texas. Fr. Mark is also part of Food for Life Television Ministry.

Connect with the Companions of the Cross online!

companionscross.org | Discover the spirituality, brotherhood and mission of the Companions of the Cross and how you can participate

vocations.companionscross.org | Explore a vocation to the priesthood with the Companions of the Cross

Like us on Facebook

COMPANIONS OF THE CROSS:
facebook.com/companionsofthecross

Follow us on Twitter

COMPANIONS OF THE CROSS:
twitter.com/CompanionsCross

Subscribe to our YouTube channel

youtube.com/user/CompanionsCross

COMPANIONS OF THE CROSS

We are a Roman Catholic community of priests, committed
to living and ministering together as brothers in the Lord.
God has called us to labour boldly for the renewal of the Church through a dynamic
evangelization centered upon Christ crucified, who is God's power and wisdom.
Spurred on by the love of God, we desire all people to come into the fullness of life
through a personal and ongoing encounter with Jesus Christ.

SPIRITUALITY

LOVE FOR CHRIST CRUCIFIED, A SPIRITUALITY OF GOD'S
POWER AND WISDOM | Jesus's death on the cross and resurrection saved the
world. Therefore, we fully commit ourselves
to him; seek his will in all we do; and trust in his power to do it.

BROTHERHOOD

LOVE FOR ONE ANOTHER, A LIFE OF TRUE BROTHERHOOD
We base ourselves on the model of Jesus and his disciples, who lived together, minis-
tered together, and supported one another.

MISSION

LOVE FOR THE CHURCH, A MISSION OF EVANGELIZATION
AND RENEWAL | We invite all people into an initial and ongoing encounter with
Jesus. As we are transformed by his love, we bring about authentic renewal in the
Church and world.

 Companions of the Cross

199 Bayswater Avenue, Ottawa, ON Canada K1Y 2G5 | 1.866.885.8824
1949 Cullen Blvd, Houston, TX USA 77087-3553 | 1.866.724.6073

WWW.COMPANIONSCROSS.ORG

Made in the USA
Middletown, DE
21 March 2017